THE MAINTENANCE
OF THE
SHIMMY-SHAMMY

CHRISTOPHER CITRO

PRAISE

Christopher Citro may be the love child of poet Russell Edson and *The Twilight Zone*. Now, you may protest that men and TV programs don't mate and produce offspring. Yet I submit that in Mr. Citro's oddball, deadpan, beguiling fables such a coupling would be business as usual. A man gently slips smoke rings over a woman's wrist like bracelets. A kid finds himself psychically stuck in the Middle Ages, as contemporary life churns around him (leading to the great phrase "trial by Jell-O"). A couple unearths a circus in their backyard. Citro's speakers' gee whiz, small town innocence is the perfect mindset/ weapon to carry into the mutating world he creates for them. Accustomed versions of reality disintegrate in that world. From the ashes of domesticity and order a new American surrealism blooms, in which the charming, the unsettling, and the strange colonize the quote unquote normal.

—Amy Gerstler

There's a fun-house effect to these poems that begins to feel deadly, or certainly dead-on, a spirited humor that pulls the scab off our droopy American moment. Could we be culturally asleep and not know it? Every art needs constant renewal—fresh eyes, a fresh voice, an original mind at work. Christopher Citro's skilled and wisely silly book goes a long way toward renewing poetry. This is a much-welcomed and necessary kick in the pants, chock-full of quirks and delights.

—Maurice Manning

Christopher Citro's masterful debut, *The Maintenance of the Shimmy-Shammy*, is part circus and part menagerie, where the 21st century quotidian rubs shoulders with boundless imagination: the figures on a ceramic Amphora come to life with an old woman eating an Egg McMuffin and a guy at the supermarket shouting into his cell phone, a family of robots move to town, a man gets a zombie replica of his own face as a gift, a therapist prescribes fireplaces to his patients. Imagination and communication drive these poems—"What? What Is It You're Trying To Tell Me?" this book asks over and over, and Citro answers with wind-up chattering teeth as a perfect metaphor for our endless difficulties in bridging the gap between feeling and saying. Christopher Citro is a poetry pirate, plundering language and image to get at the human heart, in these luminous, inventive poems.

—Erika Meitner

Christopher Citro's *The Maintenance of the Shimmy-Shammy* is simultaneously hilarious and terrifying, full of an antic wisdom and wit that insists on resilience over annihilation and despair. The remarkable imagination at work in these beautifully rendered poems shakes up the humdrum offering enlivening perspectives. These fables, these dancing lessons show us that "It's not the world, but how one orients oneself towards things..." A gathering of marvelous excavations, Citro unearths wonder re-enchanting the suburbatron of the heart. Read and experience these wild, shrewd, philosophical poems and let your world be transformed."

—Catherine Bowman

THE MAINTENANCE
OF THE
SHIMMY-SHAMMY

CHRISTOPHER CITRO

STEEL TOE BOOKS BOWLING GREEN, KENTUCKY

ISBN 978-0-9863575-0-3

STEEL TOE BOOKS
Western Kentucky University
Department of English
1906 College Heights Blvd. #11086
Bowling Green, KY 42101-1086
steeltoebooks.com

COVER ART
Marie Rosen, Untitled, 2012, oil on panel 90 x 70 cms. Courtesy of
the artist, Rossicontemporary, Brussels and the owners. Photo:
Charlotte Delval, Private Collection, Brussels.

COVER AND BOOK DESIGN
Molly McCaffrey

STEEL TOE BOOKS is affiliated with Western Kentucky University.

For Sarah

I was a fool for a girl with a dainty lexicon.

—MICHAEL CHABON, *THE MYSTERIES OF PITTSBURGH*

Wedgwood, who was to trade and commerce in many ways what
Samuel Johnson blip blip was to literature, was troubled in his
younger days blot by some kind of circulatory complaint blip blip in
one leg. If he happened to knock it against anything blot it swelled up
and put him blip blip blippity blot in bed for a few days blot...

—PAUL VIOLI, "SUMMER READING INTERRUPTED BY RAIN"

CONTENTS

ONE

TWO

THREE

ONE

STILL LIFE WITH PLUMS

The arenas of his greatness were the tabletops in his small studio.
—PETER SCHJELDAHL ON GIORGIO MORANDI

In my apartment I make my paintings. A vase—
long white neck with a thick lip—I set beside
a squat white bowl. I try cherries in the bowl.
I take the cherries away. I try two plums—
two lovers for the bowl. I remove the plums.
I try, in desperation one Sunday afternoon,
a single muskmelon. For days it sits there
bloated in the bowl. I haven't the heart to admit
I put it there in the first place by moving it.
But I do. During a rainstorm, I do.
I drop the melon from a window overlooking the street.
I do not watch it land but turn and see
the perfect empty bowl beside the long white vase.
And then I paint, one week, two weeks.
When it's finished, I let the painting dry
while I go out and walk around the town.
I wave at shopkeepers; I sit in the park
and read newspapers. Back in my apartment,
I take the painting from the easel, place it
along a wall, against a stack of others.
Turning back, I see the vase, the bowl
across the room on their little table.
Sunlight. I take a step towards—

IN THIS REALITY, YOU EXIT AT THE NEXT MCDONALD'S FOR FRIES AND A SHAKE

Somewhere in some alternate universe, there's a reality where you do get off at the next exit just to photograph the red barn. You're not a professional, but why should you let that stop you from taking a good, artsy picture now and then? Who knows, maybe you're an outsider artist and don't even know it? And even the professionals have to start somewhere. If you don't end up with a picture you can sell, at least you'll have something to show friends when they're over the house getting tanked on margaritas. It's a pleasant thing to show someone a photograph you took yourself. You watch the lines on her face soften. A smile blooms. She looks from the photo to you, then back to the photo, and you can see in her eyes that you're somehow more than you were before.

OPENING THE SHADES

One day during recess, the second grader wandered over to an empty corner of the playground. A few thistle weeds marked the crumbling edge of the tarmac. It was a sunny afternoon. He felt okay. The sandwich his mom packed for his lunch was filling and pleasant. The celery was good, too. He sat on the edge of the pavement with his legs crossed in front of him. It felt good to have legs. He wondered how long he'd known that but not known that he knew it. Probably for longer than he'd known what an oil tanker was. Maybe not for as long as he'd known about milk.

A little breeze came up from the woods nearby, and the boy began to pick at the edge of the black top. It came apart in different sized chunks. Under the third or fourth piece, the boy found a sliver of darkness. He reached down and picked it up. It felt like a raisin there pinched between his fingers. He looked down around him and didn't see any more bits of darkness. He looked up and didn't see anyone watching him, so he slipped the piece of darkness into the front pocket of his jeans. It felt warm against his leg. He thought to himself, This is the kind of thing someone could guard carefully and carry around for the rest of their lives. It'd almost be like being secretly a pirate. He decided to do just that. It was the earliest in what became a series of excellent decisions he'd make in his swashbuckling life.

PLENTY OF ROOM HERE UNDER THE BIG TOP

The old man who lives behind our house
told us this was where the traveling circus used to sleep.
We smiled and believed him—but only a little
Until, while digging in the backyard for a petunia bed,
I hit the elephant's back with the shovel.
Carefully I bent down to clear dark soil
from the wide, pale forehead. I called to you
where you were prying dandelions out of the lawn
with a steak knife. And you came running.
(The woman I love.) You leapt into the hole with me
and together we dug and scraped away to get
down to the elephant's feet, its ruby sandals glinting
in the bright spring light. Now and then,
I'd look over and catch a glimpse of your breasts
shiny with sweat and dusted with soil inside your
black tank top. You, too busy digging to notice,
clearing a stray hair from your eyes now and then.
It took hours and hours, but there she was,
ten feet below the lemonade sweating on our porch:
one perfect elephant preserved somehow just for us,
leather headdress encrusted with gold and precious stones.
I looked at you, almost unrecognizable now
for soil, and you smiled at me—teeth showing
like jewels through the dirt. I climbed out of our hole
and reached for you. You took my hand.

YOU WASH, I'LL RINSE

The tablets caused no effect whatsoever.
We took two of them before bed, kissed each other
on the tip of the nose, reclined back pulling the blankets to our chin.
Then seepy-bobos—and nothing. Jocelyn woke the next day
still a clerk at the savings and loan. I woke still the guy
who has to clean out the monkey cages down at the petting zoo.
I don't even know why the zoo has those monkeys,
it's not like a kid can pet them.
One tried once and got a pinky finger torn right off.
I found the monkey waving it at the kid through the bars—
he'd stuck the red end between the middle knuckles of his fist
and he was waving it up and down. I smacked the monkey
on the side of the head (I'm allowed—there's a sign that says),
picked up the finger, packed it in Eskimo Bars,
and we got the screaming boy into an ambulance.
Then I had to calm the goats down.
The shouting makes them bleat in unison and run in circles.
A second grader with blue bows in her hair
was waving a candy wrapper at the goats shouting,
"Stop that! Stop that! Stop that!" The goats kept at it.
I saw a llama in the next paddock start to look jumpy.
I went into gear. Then later that night, Jocelyn rubbed
ointment into the bite marks as I did the same for hers.
Mutual assistance and the remedy. And with a hopeless
gesture of faith, she placed another tablet on my tongue.
I looked at her—damp hairs around her forehead,
that little button nose—and she opened her mouth
to show me one on hers, just beginning to dissolve.
We washed each down with kiss juice and pulled the covers up again.

Hope, the thing with feathers, put out the light
by breaking the bulb with its beak.

(THIS TOWN IS) BARELY MANAGING
TO HOLD IT TOGETHER

The open season opened today.
No one knew what to do about it.

It's an open season on open seasons,
said someone at a lunch cart
to someone else at the lunch cart.

Okay, said the someone else.
She held her hotdog against her chest
defensively.

The mustard made a little mark on her lapel.
If it had been catsup,
that would have been too much.

THE WRESTLING COACH TAUGHT US HEALTH

The chapter on drugs are bad for you
showed a guy driving a convertible down a street
with the trees curling over, turning into rainbow faces.
This made me want to do drugs.
Robyn ran out of the room during *The Miracle of Life*
when the baby's head appeared between
the mommy's big white thighs. First all you could see
was a wet black bunch of hair, and then
the top of a head in there—the crown—and then
screaming from the movie screen, then a flood
as Robyn ran out of the room—a flash of hall light
as the door opened and shut. Another girl threw up
as I wondered why Robyn took off even though
she regularly bragged about having sex at parties,
didn't even try to hide the cigarettes in her purse at lunch,
and probably smoked cocaine or whatever it was they did.
Her boyfriends locked each other inside lockers
then beat against the door as if that weren't bad enough.
Her boyfriend that week was Jonathan with stringy blond hair,
a sneer, and no lights behind his eyes, not even
when he first came to our school two years ago.
He showed up used up. Now Robyn's used up.
She's not even pretty anymore. Her hair's stringy.
I wonder where she ran to when she ran out of Health?
I wonder if she's pretending to herself that she could be
disturbed by that baby's bright head popping out
in the middle of the movie screen. It's not
like it could have been a surprise. It's not
like we didn't see it coming. Mister Burke

even warned us about what we would see,
giving anyone who wanted to chicken out
a chance to leave before he turned out the lights.

SWORD SWALLOWERS IN TRANSITION

What we do is get together in a room
and just sort of talk. We get into issues.
Last week, we discussed how we felt about
string theory, but really we weren't talking
about string theory at all. One man burst
into tears when someone mentioned the tenth
dimension. He began relating this lost
memory—he was four years old, at a carnival
with his father. A man in a lion suit
pranced around, his fur matted
with sawdust. He smelled of stale sweat.
This lion-man ran up to him
waving his paws about. The boy
began to cry, but the lion kept at it—
probably he couldn't think of anything
else to do—the sobs coming in
gasping waves. His dad ran to a stall,
grabbed a pirate sword, and stabbed
the lion in the armpit. He fell dead
at the boy's feet. A lady watching
from the candy apple stand clapped.
We clapped too, then elected this guy
head of the group.

THOSE DARING OLD MEN

What I say is, it's Doug's right to get wings attached to his motorcycle if he wants them. What can they hurt? They're only a foot or so long; it's not like they'll stick out into oncoming traffic. Worse they'll do is nick up a few curbs here and there. When he first got that bike, I said to myself, "Here's Doug's mid-life boom-boom." But it was amazing to watch how happy he became. I remember when he bought that old leather helmet and the white aviator scarf. I thought, Well at least it's this and not diddling his secretary. I asked him, "So, what if you crash?" And he said, "I'd be the happiest grease spot on the boulevard, Frank." And I can respect that. Life's too precious to slowly waste away protecting it year after year. In some way, he was a lesson to us all, an unspoken example to keep climbing a rope of dreams...with a knot in it...on a ladder...of life...at sunset—or something like that. I'm no Shakespeare. But he had the right idea. And so I say now, if the guy wants to add wings to his motorcycle, why not? My own recent deep sea diving expeditions have taught me this much: dreams are like sharks. If they lose a tooth, they go ahead and grow a few goddamn more.

IF YOU MUST KNOW

The reason I carry this shovel is you just never know. Like at the bank—I'm waiting in line twenty minutes to learn that I'm in the wrong line. The teller told me this then looked me in both eyes while her lips played dead at me. I was supposed to be in a little alcove off to the left where the windows let in the light off the snow, making the *National Geographics* glow like gold-framed windows to wonderful. I had no idea. I was afraid to look in case a version of me was sitting there already, the clever me with leather shoes and nice slacks, who knew all along that's where I belonged. Thank goodness for this shovel I'd have thoughtfully brought with me and which I'd slam into the carpet there and then, digging up heaps of floorboards, concrete, spitting electric vines, gravel, pale orange soil, as the bank and that teller's lips parachuted into the air above me and I dropped into a different, if darker, universe where things make some kind of sense.

A SEA VOYAGE AND THE ATTENDANT PERSPECTIVE

The beavers built a dam at the foot of our bed,
and now the mattress is beginning to float.
I reach out to put my arm around you,
knowing you're prone to seasickness
as we begin to bob and tip. A seagull passes
low across the headboard. When I see them
in the parking lot down at the mall,
they seem unpleasant, like flying rats.
How odd, I say as I reach to bring my other arm
around you, how majestic they are
when seen in their proper environment.

FOR WE, THE WIDE AWAKE

The backyard at night, powdered bone
spread from porch to picnic table.
The sky as blue as noon, clouds even
white with shimmering edges, the sort
out of which birds fly. Being night,
only bats emerge, swarming space,
bringing a darkness to dark,
clearing the air of stinging insects,
of moths, peeking into curtained windows,
looking for us—I'm guessing—
as we lie awake in bed talking in circles.
"Is that not a robin's peek and tut?" "Is that
a bluebird, a cooling breeze of jasmine?"

A THEME SONG THAT NEVER GETS OLD

We keep a bear above our bed.
We like it up there, mounted in attack stance—
shoulders hunched, claws raised, eyes
satanic, lips folded back revealing
black gums and teeth. What teeth!
Julie and I are startled by those teeth every night
of our lives, and we've been under
the bear for going on eight years now.
Gurgle goes the mouthwash,
soap on our faces, flush the toilet, and crawl
under the covers. A kiss on the tip
of each other's nose, lie back and look up
at the bear hanging above our bed.
Scream a little, then sleep eventually.

ONLY BETTER (BLACK MOTHS)

Each time Jimmy disappears into his cave he comes out later with an even more beautiful one. The last, it was six inches across, deep blue, almost black, and when you got close, a complete cosmos of pinpricks of light opened up across the velvet. I thought I saw a shooting star; it crossed from one wing to the other silently, leaving a trail of glitter. I wanted to make a wish, and I trusted Jimmy enough to do it right there in front of him. I closed my eyes and said to myself in the hollow of my skull, "I wish exactly what *is* happening *were* happening right this moment." Before I opened my eyes, I leaned in forward and kissed the body between the glittering wings. When I opened and stood back, Jimmy looked into my right eye and then into my left. Then after a moment's stillness, he disappeared back inside his cave. Two weeks later, it all happened again.

OUR APPLE TREES

Following a deer path along the tree line,
we stumble upon a refuse pit so old
the tin cans appear actually made of tin,
glass medicine bottles, buckets dissolved
into lace. These trees, you wonder,
must have been protection—horses
leaning down from the fence for what
they might reach on the ground.
The branches forming a square, reaching
around a house that may have stood here,
a house some man might have built
at the edge of this field so his wife
and he could watch over their alfalfa.
And the woman planted, one each corner,
a pip from a store-bought Jonathan.
In a few summers, they had no need
for town. As the year's light bronzed,
apples would bang onto their roof, roll
along the smooth grooves, fall
into their upraised hands
as they sat in rocking chairs
like some kind of emperors
watching the sunlight pick out
a pink sheen across the autumn milo.

CERAMIC AMPHORA, EARLY 21ST CENTURY, ATHENS, OHIO

Someone should paint clay jugs nowadays
with people on the outside, only
they should be our people, they should be us
today. A few could be wearing togas and
chasing one another with spears and erections,
because I'm sure that sort of thing still goes on.
But there should also be a guy in the supermarket
standing in front of the spaghetti sauce shouting
into a cell phone he's holding against his right ear
with his left hand, a thirteen year old walking
down the street playing an electric guitar
that's not plugged in, a toddler with lights
in her shoes, an old woman eating
an Egg McMuffin, a baby underneath
one of those walkie-talkie monitors. On
the opposite side of the vase could be
the parents sitting with their knees splayed
toward the observer, the other
squawk box on an end table next to the couch.
Their heads are thrown back
against the cushions, their mouths open
as two baby birds waiting to be fed,
two tired clay vessels.

NEW YEAR'S RESOLUTION TBA

On the coldest night of the year I heard him huffing and puffing out there through the storm windows and the regular windows. I peeked through the curtains and what to my wondering eyes did appear but some furry guy with no clothes on doing pirouettes over by the begonia bush. I made as if to call out to Margaret, but instantly thought better. What if, instead of gawking at the silliness, she took a fancy to this guy and his loopy bravado? It wasn't that I felt threatened exactly, just backed into one of those corners into which a man gets pushed. And of course there was little time to consider before action would be required. I could plainly hear Margaret in the kitchen making coming-into-the-TV-room-with-low-salt-microwave-popcorn sounds, and she'd see soon enough for herself. In this upcoming scene, what role would there be for me? As I saw the man roll across the frosty grass and leap into a sort of swan shape, but a very masculine kind of swan with broad beating wings, outthrust chest and pounding feet, I slipped into action. I—

I'M CAUGHT, KEEP AWAY

When traveling in the land where they eat the songbirds have care.
If, while climbing a lemon tree to get that much closer
to the clouds, your hand sticks to an adhesive switch
concealed in the leaves, try not to call out.
Instead assume a low warble as if to console
yourself, while warning others away.
Under the magnifying sun, carry on for hours
if need be, until the man who set the trap
weeks ago—a porcupine of them
on his plum red moped's back—returns.
He'll see you up there from a long way down the road
standing out against the barley fields, you
in your blue windbreaker, corduroys, with hiking book
in the top branches. When he calls to you
from the path, merely babble back.
When he shouts at you from directly below,
one arm against the trunk, warble a lower tone.
Deep sounds carry the farthest, wide valleys
of invisible waves over fields toward the distant hills.
He'll likely grow tired and, muttering, put-put away.
If he tries to climb up after you, the moment
his hand touches your leg, kick. Kick hard.

YOU CAN ALWAYS BUY A NEW DRESS

It's like what they tell you to do
if your dress catches on fire.
Stop, drop and roll.

Stop. Don't pick up the phone.
Drop. Hit the floor—
do like a corpse does—but then roll.

Roll like you did when you were a kid
and all innocent and happy
and you whirled around the house,
steamrolling until you puked.

Then keep rolling,
even if you knock over furniture.
Roll until you hit a wall, then
roll in the other direction.

Keep this up until the thought
of calling your ex-boyfriend to see
if he might want to come over
or something
for some coffee
or something
falls out of your head.

NO, I WILL NOT BE YOUR GIRLFRIEND

The human heart is on the left side of the chest, not in the middle of the ribcage where it seems it should be. There is a balance to the body, after all. If you have two of something, they'll be evenly spaced on each side of a line drawn down your middle, for example your arms, feet and nipples. If there's only one of something, it'll be right smack in the middle on that line, like the nose, the mouth, the belly button. So the heart, since we each have only one, should be in the middle of the chest, behind the sternum. This, however, is not the case. Evolutionary biologists figure that the sternum is a structural weak point, the joining of the bones of the rib cage. Things are most likely to break at a joint—imagine a falling boulder, a kick from a mastodon, a spear tip. So, evolution must have selected for people whose hearts were a little to one side of this vulnerable area. Time goes on, this effect becomes greater, and today our heart is to be found securely on the left side of our chest, behind a safe, unbroken wall of ribs. This is a good idea from the standpoint of the preservation of life. As well, it illustrates the innate ability of the human heart to get out of the way of danger.

SURE, YOU ALWAYS LAND ON YOUR FEET

But why are you always
falling out of windows in the first place?

STOP DOING THAT

I can't take you anywhere anymore. Last week, we went to the opera. The next day you wrote one. Do you have any idea how annoying that is? After our trip to Cape Canaveral (the last time I remember being truly happy), there you were burrowed down in a pile of recycling in the back yard. Two weeks later, a rumble woke me up in bed. Was it you bringing me the paper and my pipe? Well, no. It was you lifting off. Did you enjoy your little trip around the moon? Some of us never get to see the other side ourselves. We have to rely on other people to tell us just how dark it is.

TWO

HELP! I'M FLOATING!

Two weeks of taking these little white pills
and you're free.
You'll be immune to gravity any time you want.
Just by saying to yourself, "I quit,"
up you'll float. Fly around the room.
Shoot over to Paris and back.
Dive bomb your enemies. Whatever you want.
Then all you have to do is say to yourself, "I'm back,"
and you'll land and stick to the earth as usual.
They represent a wonderful advancement, these pills.
Much better than the ones I used to take
to make me invisible.
I'd get so terribly depressed wondering why
no one ever talked to me.
Then I'd remember.

SCIENCE FICTION FAMILY

Imagine that a family of robots moves into town, arriving from Texas in a beat-up car. Born in a factory that looked like a big metal box: a mom robot, a dad and two children robots. Somehow they developed consciousness, petitioned for their rights to self-determination and won them from a local magistrate. Ready to start a new life of their own, the family moves into your town one quiet day in November.

They rent a small place above a toiletries shop on Main Street to set up their simple household. The father robot gets a job in a factory making mouthwash; the mother works from home proofreading legal documents. The children are enrolled in the local elementary school and test among the highest in their respective classes. The family puts its surname upon its mailbox and installs heavy-duty electrical out-lets in every room.

Imagine what the neighbors would say. Picture the expression on the face of the middle-aged widow living down the hall. Imagine the attitude of the clerk behind the counter of the corner store. Put yourself in the place of the youngest child as she stands on the playground one gray day all alone in the center of a circle of silent second graders.

EMILY, IT'S BETTER THIS WAY

They landed in the morning and nothing happened.
It was six hours before the hatch split.

When finally they emerged, we strained to see
faces, but their helmet visors were mirrored—

we looked and pointed and saw ourselves.
The spacemen lumbered out, bounced around

on the lawn like great big children
in silver snow suits, dancing in slow motion.

Then the sirens blew and we knew
the tornadoes were coming. The sky went

green and we headed for cover. The last person
to see the spacemen was Emily. Before ducking

into the shelter, she looked back and saw one
begin to lift off into the sky. Another spaceman

tried to hold that one down, but he lost his footing
and both of them shot into angry clouds.

HOMESCHOOLING IS REALLY TAKING OFF

Hallways shake with the muffled buffet
of nothing echoing back from nothing.
Paint bubbles from cinderblock walls
until even from outside it sounds as if
a herd of mastodons (extinct) are about
to tear the place down from the inside out.
No one's out there to hear, though.
Just one car in the lot, a blue Volkswagen.
In an office whose door never opens,
sits the Principal of The Great Unknown
Elementary School—hunched over a crystal set,
sending recorded samples of the silence
into the sky, the dark matter, the something
in the nothingness scientists tell us
must be up there for the everything else
that is something, what little there is of it,
not to come crashing in on itself.
And for any second graders
who may have lost their way up there.

COWBOYS WON'T CUT IT ANYMORE

The day after the circus came to town,
it suddenly disappeared.
One minute there was a sweet-smelling cloud
floating over Main Street—citizens
pointing to the sky, taking deep breaths,
scowling, but taking more deep breaths—
and then there was nothing again.
The same nothing there always was.

Tom Bradley tried to cheer us all up
by pointing at the neon sign above his five-and-dime—
the moving image of a cowboy taking off his hat
and then putting it back on again—
but no one bought it. We were a people
used to living without lions and cotton candy,
then we got used to living with lions and cotton candy,
then we had to get used to nothing again.

BEING NECESSARY FOR THE MAINTENANCE
OF THE SHIMMY-SHAMMY

We built a hut just for the jukebox. Above it we hung little lights on a string. At night the girls gather there to sip iced cocktails and shake about to the music. It really is pleasant. Occasionally the lions come down from the hills and try to crawl into the hut. We let them at first, but then they carried away one of the girls. We were all night out looking for her. Finally she was discovered halfway down a tunnel in the side of the mountain where our god lives. So we said, "No more!" Now any time the lions come up to the hut as it twinkles and wobbles in the night, we have guys whose job it is to beat them back with big sticks. Lately, they've made a thing out of hitting the lions in time with the tunes on the jukebox. The girls seem to appreciate this; they shake themselves even more energetically.

TEN MORE MINUTES, PLEASE

The Williams are coming home any day now. We're going to have to face up to it and do something about the living room rug. Last night's party may have finally finished it off. House-sitting for the neighbors is supposed to be a sacred trust, like knighthood or dog-walking. Keep the houseplants watered, the cat's litter box emptied; don't put the cordless phone in the microwave to try to call up the big bang or use the electric can opener to carve a map of the night sky into the dining room table. We're going to have to burn the photo we took of ourselves two weeks ago—back when we were young in our Williams-hood and the future looked endless and paved with soft bricks of joy—smiling on the front lawn with *The Williams* written underneath in cursive. We have to cancel the magazine subscriptions and tell the church group not to send over that exchange student from Japan. We've got to go back to being our plain old, non-Williams selves.

WE BLEW IT AND NOW WE PAY

After the scientists discovered the fluorescent paint under our bed, they left in disgust. We'd strung them along as far as was possible. From the day we first placed the call to the Institute about the species of butterfly we'd discovered in our garage, we couldn't move for the wall-to-wall scientists. How we loved and cherished them. Nothing brightens up a dull existence like a fascinated audience. When they tested our toothpaste—after you told them it could be used to stop time—I felt both gratified and a little afraid. When the tests proved the toothpaste ordinary, a tide began to turn—the scientists somewhat hesitant to rush up to the roof with you the next night to investigate your discovery of a pterodactyl lodged in the chimney. When all they found was a dead pigeon on which you'd glued two palpably false six-foot wings, that seemed to finish things off for good. When you announced the next day that our bedroom was full of glow worms, I knew it was all over.

THIS YEAR'S WILL BE THE LAST

The traveling fair pulled into town and set up in the flats where the trains used to come through. There's only a few clapboard shacks down there now. The fair turned them into haunted houses. You can go into Ray's old mechanic shop, Ray's House of Doom now, and still see him standing in the back by his work table. A single bulb illuminating half his body, his denim shirt, the wrench in his left hand and a nearly invisible drop of blood at the left corner of his mouth. It's the grown-ups scream loudest at this. The kids ride the rickety roller coaster set up by the old railroad tracks, the grown-ups visit Ray and come out shrieking, reaching for the ground even before they sit down on it, hug themselves and sway.

CUCKOLD AT THE ZOO

She allowed the buffalo to
put his head in her lap.

His curly hair, his
worry and grandeur.

A hump in his back and
the cock beneath his bulk.

No wonder her husband
threw peanuts, then the peanut machine.

IF ONLY I'D THOUGHT OF IT

Her whole family hates smoking.
She told me one day window-shopping
for puppies. I had one going at the time,
and she said, "My whole family really
hates smoking." I nodded and said,
"Okay." I didn't really know what that meant,
though. Did they sit around the dinner table
taking turns saying: "It's a nasty habit." "Yes,
a nasty habit." "Such a nasty habit."
"Don't they have any respect for their bodies?"
They must have been pretty committed.
And so was Mona. And so
she dumped me. Then, get this,
Matt says he sees her out
the next night with another guy—
and this one's got a cigarette in his face.
I couldn't believe it when he told me.
The guy was blowing smoke rings as they sat
alone together at a café. Then he reached out,
grabbed the rings and placed them
over Mona's hands like bracelets.
I could have done that.

A LITTLE QUANTUM PHYSICS CAN BE DANGEROUS

"Are you willing to live in a house with a green couch?"
Mona asked. "Is that the sort of man I married?"
Michael looked at Mona and did not reply.
He knew this was one of those decisive moments
that sometimes occur between two people.
He didn't want to say the wrong thing
and have to live the rest of his life in a universe
where he messed up. He wanted to say the answer
that would blossom inside his woman
like a bouquet of daises. Then he'd only have
to visit the other universe—the wrong one—sometimes
at night in his sleep. It would be a dismal place
with fear running through it like a greasy black ribbon.
When he'd wake from that universe, he'd mumble
that he'd had a nightmare and Mona would hold him
close to her bare breasts. She'd caress his hair, and he'd
calm down—awake in the right universe, in a house
of love. A house with a couch in it whose color
Michael couldn't for the life of him see clearly
from the back of this furniture store in the soon-to-be
past, gritting his teeth with the effort to decide.

THEY MUST BAKE AN AWFUL LOT OF CAKES

Try venturing out beyond the searchlights and see where it gets you. I remember when it was Gerry out venturing beyond the searchlights to see where it'd get him. Remember we didn't hear from him for two weeks and that greasy black smoke covered the playground right next to the searchlights for a whole afternoon? And then we hear Gerry crawling down the street one evening when all the rest of us were home eating Sunday dinner, and even when he'd been sitting on his own couch for an hour with a drink and soothing music on the hifi, even then he couldn't do anything except stare straight ahead with his mouth open. Even when Judith from next door—remember how they always used to be borrowing cups of sugar back and forth from each other all the time—even when she put his head between her breasts and blew gently at his receding hairline, close up as she was, even then all Gerry could muster was a sort of high-pitched whine at the back of his throat like you'd make if you were playing dolls and the princess just found out her prince was devoured by beasts while in the jungle fighting for her honor. Gerry wasn't fighting for anyone's honor when he ventured out beyond the searchlights that night. Not even Judith's honor. He was already getting a cup of her sugar practically every other night. What more did he want?

APPARENTLY, I'M NOT A JOINER

When I asked if she was planning on attending
the manager's complementary Bar-B-Q,
she said she hadn't decided yet. It was to be held
in the little gazebo at the south end of the hotel,
just across from the swamp. "Are you?"
she asked, then answered her own question
with, "Of course, you're not. You're not a joiner."
The elevator door opened, she walked out
and I stood there. The door closed and the elevator
headed for the third floor. The door opened
at the third floor. It stayed open a few seconds,
then it closed. The elevator returned to the first floor.
Some strangers got on. They smiled at me,
so I smiled at them. They got off on the second floor.
I stayed on. The elevator went up to the third floor.
A man got on with a suitcase. He didn't smile at me,
so I didn't smile at him. He got off on the first floor.
This went on for a while until I got self-conscious.
I rode to my floor, went to my room and closed the door.
I locked the door. I unlocked it, then locked it
again. I listened closely and appreciated
the subtle music of that sound.

INSIDE THE ROBOT THERE'S ANOTHER ROBOT

The robot had stopped singing even though
we'd replaced the batteries that morning.
"That's the second set in a week. That robot's had it."
At this, Jeremy leapt out of bed, grabbed Jeremy Junior by the throat—
Jeremy Senior doesn't know I call the robot Jeremy Junior
(I only call him Jeremy Junior in my mind,
where I also call Jeremy Senior Jeremy Senior)—
and flung him across the room in the direction of the cactus tree.
"Who puts a cactus tree in a bedroom?" I asked
when Jeremy first brought it home—he was just Jeremy then—
and he said, "I do. It looks the same if it's alive or dead,
so you don't have to remember to water it." Which I did.
I remembered to water it for a couple years. Then I forgot.
And Jeremy was right, it looks the same. The only way
you can tell it's long past dead is the little puff of soil smoke
when the robot's head hit the pot. As if this were
some kind of magic smoke, the kind they have in movies,
out of this cloud we saw the robot break open
and another, smaller robot pop out.
This one looked like a miniature version of Jeremy Junior,
only with redder cheeks and, I think, freckles.
Rising, unsteadily at first, to his feet he wobbled over to our bed,
stood straight with his arms by his side, tilted his head back
and began to sing. Like a little bird saying thank you to the sun,
that clear tone floated over Jeremy and me as we fell
into each other's arms. Jeremy Senior happy again.
Jeremy the Third singing. And me in there too, someplace,
thinking of things inside my head.

KEEP IT UP AND YOU'LL FREEZE LIKE THAT

A family that dresses up as clowns together stays together. At least, that was Father's idea. So he bought costumes for himself, his wife, and his young son and daughter. They didn't take them off for two days. The father wore his to the office. The wife wore hers to the grocery and a PTA meeting. The boy played shortstop in polka dots. The little girl in the purple wig had tea parties with teddy bears and a stuffed owl the family inherited when Grandfather died. After two days, Father decided they'd had enough. Together at the dinner table, he said, "We've had our fun." That was when they discovered they couldn't get the costumes off. The slap shoes were as if glued to their feet, the baggy jumpsuits made from steel fabric with no zippers or buttons. The oil paints wouldn't wash away, no matter what solvent they tried. In their panic, they pulled at each other's red noses until they lifted one another off the floor.

WHAT? WHAT IS IT YOU'RE TRYING TO TELL ME?

She keeps bringing home those teeth, the ones that chatter when you wind them up. Their gums are bright red, like nobody's gums in real life. I don't know where she's getting them from. This town used to be full of magic supply stores—every other window downtown had collapsible top hats, inflatable doves—but that was the old days. Yet there she is arriving home with shopping bag after shopping bag bursting with those chattering teeth. The living room's the only place left in the house where you can sit down without fear of getting a nip. And even after all the discussions we've had, just last night she comes home with another two bags. She sat next to me on the sofa, wound one up and set it on her knee there between us. When she let it go, it started away chattering. Chat-a-chat-a-chat-a-chat-a. She looked up at me, smiling, with her eyes open, expectant.

COMMUNICATION PROBLEMS IN THE MIDDLE AGES

In the Middle Ages, I had not yet learned how to ride a bicycle.
And so I was sad, as anyone would be who had to walk everywhere.
I'd see the other kids tooling off in packs down the street,
off to adventures like smoking and kissing girls
and telling dirty stories or breaking windows,
and I'd have to stay stuck in the mud in my front yard.
In the Middle Ages, most people were stuck in the mud
and they never got clean unless it rained
while they were carrying rocks or digging for roots in a ditch
or else someone threw them into a river.
Sometimes they threw people into ponds to see if they were a witch.
Everyone knows this. It's not news anymore.
Everyone also knows the joke about if they drowned
they were a witch and if they floated they dragged them back out
and burned them at the stake as a witch. That's not even funny anymore.
And it wasn't back in the Middle Ages either. I saw one or two people
get burned at the stake. I thought about trying to put out the fire,
but I'd only have been grounded and sent to my room without dessert.
In the Middle Ages this was known as trial by Jell-O.
I also saw more than one or two people drown in the pond.
They probably thought it was a better way to go
than being tied to a pole and set fire to. Either way,
they knew it was all over as soon as someone grabbed hold of them.
In the Middle Ages, my mom used to grab my face
to stop me from talking when I was talking too much
and wouldn't shut up. When I'd stopped, she'd let go—
giving my mouth an extra last twist just to make sure
I'd gotten the message.

CATERPILLARS AND GRASS SNAKES

The children have pretty near taken this town over. No one gets the *New York Times* delivered to the doorstep anymore. Instead, it's that magazine with full-colored pictures of blue birds, diagrams of beaver dams, articles about how clowns go to school, and line drawings of backyards with secret discoveries to find and circle in pencil—a badger in the BBQ grill, a blue heron in the fence slats. In the mornings, one used to hear retirees discussing tumors over the neighborly hedges, now it's all cooing and murmurs. The word "milk" is tossed about with monotonous regularity. One hears: "If you want to be the moo cow, then I want to be the horse." "I want to be the horse." That's all there is in this town these days, moo cows, beaver dams, and cooing. We've got grownups lined up for miles outside of town, suitcases in hand, to get in.

THE PLAYGROUND IS NOT FOR YOU

The sandbox is for the kids. As are the purple swings. That duck you can sit on—also for the kids. Ditto the swirly disk and the tubes you can crawl through and see girls at the other end. All for the kids. That's why this part of the park is walled off and closed with a locked gate. The wall may be only three feet high, but that's enough. And the iron gate has a lock that can only be opened by a kid. A secret. See, observe that group of adults, the hard-hatted men with acetylene torches and full, smoked-glass face masks, the women behind them holding sledge hammers in their business suits and all-day support hose. The little old people in the rear fashioning figurines of the Andrews Sisters out of plastique explosive. They're not going to get in either.

I NEVER INTEND TO, HOW 'BOUT YOU?

It's eight o'clock. Time to plug the ladder in. I love our new ladder, the way it glows bright blue when the juice is flowing. I agree with you: our friends are no use to us anymore. I left a message on the machine saying, "Hello. Thanks for calling the so-and-so residence. Please don't do it again, though." Hopefully, that'll do the trick. I hate being interrupted when we're watching the ladder. The way it glows there, propped up in the corner... It's like it was made to be here in our house shining all night long just so we can sit and watch and tell each other all the different things we imagine we'd reach if we climbed it.

IN MY SKULL

There's a little man in a mansion
containing only one coffee table
on which he's managed to stub his toe.

SINGLE MALE SEEKS SOMEONE WHO'LL STAY

I opened the door to get the paper last Sunday, and there was a goose standing on the front step. It looked up at me, then took one step to the side making room for me to pass. So I did. What else was there to do? I walked out onto the lawn, picked up the paper, and walked back to the door. When I opened it, the goose stepped inside and waddled into the living room. I stood outside holding the door. Did a goose just walk into my house? It turned a corner and went into the hallway to the bedroom. I stepped inside. "I'm following a goose into my house," I said out loud as I did. I walked through the living room, turned into the hall just in time to see the goose fly up and out through a window I had not remembered leaving open. "And then the goose flew away," I said out loud to no one. In fact, it was at that instant that I realized finally just how empty my life was.

THREE

ALL PURPOSE, ME

I want to work in a twine factory.
I just feel it would be a comfort.
Rolling in towering beige spools,
rows of spinning machines quietly
spinning, friendly muscular ladies
lighting cigarettes off each others' cigarettes
under tightly wrapped head scarves,
slipping the finished products—
orderly rolls of household helpfulness—
into clear plastic sleeves, shrink-wrapped
into new skins, packed into
boxes and shipped around the world.
"Honey, pick up some twine while you're out."
"What kind?"
"Are there kinds?"
And hours later, someone ties back a curtain
to let the sunlight in, someone else
closes a bag of long underwear for summer storage.
A stray length floats to the floor.
The cat wants a mouse to play with.
The twine becomes a mouse.

HAPPY BIRTHDAY TO ME

"The last thing I need is a zombie with a replica of my own face," said Willy. "So you don't like your birthday present then," replied Bianca. "It isn't that," said Willy, "but what is he for, anyway? What am I supposed to do with one around the house?" "He could help with the cleaning," suggested Bianca as she waved a hand, palm open, towards the rumpus room. Willy followed her gesture: entertainment center (cobwebbed), sunken conversation pit (filled with alligators and musty water), one of those giant egg chairs you sit in while smooth music plays on the hifi (spikes all along the inside, a cobra coiled on the cushion). Without saying a word, Willy looked Bianca right in the eye. His birthday present stepped to his side and, with the same eyes (only clouded over and crusty at the edges), did the same. Willy had to stop himself putting an arm across his own shoulder.

HAVE IT YOUR WAY

"Lunchtime!" called Thommy's mom. He was in the backyard ditch playing with some action figures. There was a princess, a man in a turban and a robot missing a leg. The robot spent most of the time lying on his side. "That is your special power then," said Thommy.

The princess was in love with the man in the turban. Her name was Melody and she came from Detroit where there's an academy for princesses. The man in the turban was named Phil. He didn't love the princess. He loved his motorcycle. The Black Bandit stole his motorcycle, and Phil made a vow to get it back. The princess found this terribly romantic. The robot watched it all from his side down in the dirt. He would have made a comment but he couldn't think of anything to say, except, "I wish I could stand up straight."

"Lunchtime, Thommy! Get over here!" *She sounds like she means it this time*, thought Thommy. He climbed out of the ditch, leaving his action figures behind. While Thommy was eating his fish fingers and decaf cola, a gush of dirty water washed the princess, Phil, and the robot down into a drainage pipe. "This is a different sort of adventure," said the robot perking up. The princess and Phil were decidedly not perked up.

PREPARING PHOENIX FOR DINNER

We threw open our door
and it walked right into the kitchen.

We threw open the oven.
It stepped inside.

We turned it on to 450
and we heard a cooing and murmurs.

When we eat
we'll lose our tongues.

Then we'll grow new tongues,
better ones.

A RAISING

We gathered at Niedermeyer's house the next week.
Standing around with our hands in our back pockets,
some of us hummed, some of us kicked clods of earth
from mud ruts. Then someone—I think it was Stan,
or someone just like Stan—suggested we build
the Niedermeyers a barn. And that's what we did.
We built them a barn in the shape of a seven year old boy.
The roof was a baseball hat, the side door smelled of bubble gum.
The hayloft we made out of denim. When we'd finished—
when the last lick of paint completed the backpack and the lunch box—
we packed up our caring hearts and walked down the drive
back toward town. The last one looked back saw
Mr. and Mrs. Niedermeyer walking toward the barn
with milk and cookies on a tray. Mr. Niedermeyer
held the barn door open as Mrs. Niedermeyer
ducked her way in with the tray. Mr. Niedermeyer
followed and the barn door slammed shut.
The thump crossed the cornfields.

SHE LIFTED HER ARMS BUT SHE WASN'T SURRENDERING.

He keeps leaving
bottles
with messages for me.

He doesn't finish
the liquor though,
so the notes come out
hopelessly smudged.

I haven't understood
a word he's said
in years.

THE SALVATION OF EDNA

Who brought the Statue of Liberty cake to the Xmas party anyway? Everyone I ask says, "It wasn't me," but it didn't just materialize out of thin air on the snack table next to the photocopier. Edna was the first to slip a little square onto her plate. Next thing any of us knows, she's thrown down her empty plate and is frantically shoveling fistfuls into her face. She knocked it off the table and was reduced to rolling around on the carpet, her mouth open, blurred with gray icing behind her flapping hands. She was like an animal, a frightening yet pathetic creature. I saw one of the copy boys trying to look up her skirt as she flailed about, and I sent him away. When there was no more cake left, except a crust around her smeared mouth, Edna got up off the floor, patted down her dress and quietly walked back to her cubicle in HR as if nothing had happened. The rest of us just stood there with our eyes and mouths agape. And now, a month later, Edna still isn't really back to her old, pre-Statue of Liberty state. Nowadays she's a different woman, an absolute joy to be around.

ON TOP OF AN ALREADY LOSING PERSONALITY

It seemed Leon was finally doing better. That is, until he got that war monument. I don't know who gave it to him or what they thought they were doing. Did they think it would help him get his feet back on the ground? If so, boy, were they ever off the mark. By itself, it's fine. Pretty much your standard equestrian war memorial: a guy in a uniform waving his sword from on top of a rearing stallion. An inscription along the base reading something like: *Gone But Not Forgotten.* Fine. But the effect it's had on Leon has been anything but acceptable. There he is, every day, pulling the thing on its little wheeled trolley through town. If anyone passes by without saluting or weeping or putting their hat against their heart, he lets go of the rope and leaps upon the person. It doesn't matter who it is—a child, old ladies, the Chief of Police. The court costs and hospital bills are about to drive Leon into economic misery. To say nothing of the toll it's taken on his standing in the community. Before he got the memorial, it looked like he'd almost lived down the scandal left over from the time someone gave him the shoes that play the national anthem.

THE BEST ONE THIS TOWN EVER HAD

Before Tom came home with the toboggan, he was what you'd call, more or less, a straight-laced, regular kind of guy. You can't get much more normal than a manager at an accountant's office. That's what Tom was. An accountant. He had a desk calendar marked twelve months in advance with "cut hair" written on every third Thursday. The barbershop where he went refused to take an appointment more than one month in advance, but if they would have Tom could have penned them in up to this time next year. Like I said, Tom was a regular kind of guy. Then one day, he's suddenly carrying around a toboggan. You know, one of those long wooden sled things that curls up in the front. I mean, it hasn't snowed here in thirty-some odd years. It wouldn't have all this cactus if we did. But there he went about with this toboggan. He carried it everywhere, wouldn't put it down. To the pancake house, his son's little league, the opera. Everywhere. We finally had to elect him mayor. When we put the little gold crown on his head, then he let the damn thing go.

THE EXACT OPPOSITE OF EXILE

Sure, his methods are unorthodox. If you describe a therapist who prescribes fireplaces as unorthodox, then that he is. He prescribed a fireplace to Mrs. Johnson who came in with sexual complaints. Apparently it worked, too. Mrs. Johnson has had them installed in every room of the house. Mr. Johnson was glad to do the work. You could see him walking through the house, covered in grouting dust and wood splinters, with the biggest grin on his face. The doctor prescribed a fireplace to the Miller girl whose mother brought her to see him after she tried to take a nap in the family station wagon while it was running in the garage. The doctor told her two hours alone every night in front of a crackling blaze would do the trick. As a side prescription, he stipulated that the Miller parents must wear duct tape across their mouths during the two hours. So far, the change in the girl has been startling. She's taken up sculpture and plans on moving to the mountains to open an artist colony. He's really done some marvelous things in this town, despite his admittedly unorthodox methods. If you don't believe me, just look at his office doorstep first thing in the morning. You can't see the welcome mat for all the plates of brownies, cakes and plastic-wrapped bowls of homemade chicken soup.

DONE PLAYING HARD TO GET

There's more than one way to read that fist of hers.
It might be a defensive gesture—like carrying on
an entire conversation with your arms crossed—
but it might mean something else completely.
Maybe she's got a tiny apple in there—keeping it warm
so you can eat it later, baked in the oven of her body.
Or perhaps a single pearl found at the edge of a ballroom
her parents dragged her to when she was ten.
Her dress itched her knees so she crawled
in the shadows, stumbling upon this pale eye
escaped from some rich woman's neck.
She grabbed it, kept it secret until now, until your face,
your body, your special way of looking directly at her
when you speak. And she's about to reveal it to you
if you'll just calm down and reach out
to take both of her hands in yours.

TYPICAL, REALLY

One thousand chipmunks
woke him up from a deep sleep

and he mistook them
for angels

when he could simply have been
amazed at a thousand
chipmunks in one place.

IN TIME TO SAVE A LIFE

He bought a tin of breath mints, but to his surprise it was full of mint-sized horses. They were alive and quite energetic. Dozens and dozens of them. Miniature brown and black horses with very small manes that nevertheless gleamed in the light from his desktop lamp. When he opened the tin, a few jumped from his hand to the desk. Some galloped up into the crook of his arm and stood ruminating. The horses that had leapt to the desk found a puddle of cherry soda. From this, they drank deeply. Upon finishing, they tipped back their long heads and cleared their nostrils forcefully. Tiny as they were, thought Tommy, you'd have to describe their bearing as majestic.

FREE VERSE

He kept sneaking into supermarkets to write poetry on the fresh fruit. He used a magic marker to write stanzas on the apples stacked in pyramids, on piles of heavy oranges. A ball point pen will work on some cantaloupes. Not above the use of a stencil, he'd spray paint especially poetic words on the strawberries and cherries. *Abscond* fits nicely on an apricot. *Sirocco* can be placed along the stem of a banana and the average shopper won't know the difference. Until she gets home, that is. Then the questions come. "Why an elegy on my mango? Why a formal rhyme scheme for the coconut?" Calls to the service department ensue. Then he has to be even more sneaky in order to pull it off again. Once, a stock boy caught him by his collar and said, "Dude! What do you think you're doing with that limerick and that kiwi? You are so busted." After pushing a specially installed alarm button with his sneakers, the stock boy looked down at his clenched fist. Instead of a collar, he held a few strips of cloth and a tattered page of Emily Dickinson. All hail the smooth criminals who walk among us.

LIFESTYLE OF THE NON-QUARTERBACK
AND THE NON-CHEERLEADER

You always said that's what you loved about me. When I dumped that entire cask of olive oil over my head and rolled about on the floor of World Market saying, "I'm a kipper! Please someone tickle the kipper!" you were the only visitor I had at the station the next morning before my little visit with the judge. I'll never forget that you came to see me then. Remember, you wore that little button you'd made with your button-making machine that said: *Free Kipper Boy*. I knew when I saw you there through the two inch Plexiglas that you were the kind of woman I could consider teaming up with to take over the world. I had no idea you'd pick me up upon my release in your special, homemade rocket car. Remember the looks of jealousy on the faces of the cops as we pulled out? You gunned the engine, and we melted the arrows right off the pavement.

LOVE IS A REVOLUTIONARY ACT

Where did that potato come from?
From the potato store.
Is it nice in the potato store?
If you're comfortable around potatoes it is.
Sounds like a fine place to call home.
Most don't.
Why, I wonder?
People don't live in stores, as a rule.
Who made up all these rules?
No one, or maybe rich people.
I'm sick of all these rules.
Why are you undoing my pants?
Aren't you sick of all these rules too?

TURN DOWN THE THERMOSTAT, DARLING

Do people lost in an icy wilderness,
about to have to eat each other, ever
have sex just before they die?
Think paradoxical undressing.
Laboratory conditions in which to test this
would, admittedly, be difficult to arrange.
And test subjects thin on the ground.
Sometimes at night at home with the wife,
as we polish off another rack of lamb
with glazed onions and sit back to sip
something chardonnay or cab franc,
and she says something lilting such as
"So, what'd you do at school today, darling,"
I seize up, the wine at my lips.
But my lips can't get on with sipping.
That's one of the first signs of frostbite.
Unsippable lips. Rebellion of the lips.
And there's only one known cure for that.

A MARRIAGE MADE ON THE DINING ROOM FLOOR

"Get out of the way," said Ben to his cat. He nudged Miss Sniffles and she shifted her bulk a few inches. They were crouched together under the table in the dining room. Made of solid oak, it was the kind of table that inspired confidence. And confidence was just what Ben and Miss Sniffles lacked when a thunderstorm shook the house. Ben's wife was used to it—after two years of marriage and two before that living, as they say, in sin. She used to say that living with a man who hid under a table from thunder made her want to hide under a table herself. Ben said, "Fine. We'll make room for you, honey." She tried pointing out that oak trees are notoriously lightning prone, and so maybe hiding under an oak table in an electrical storm might not be the brightest idea. Ben said he couldn't read the encyclopedia's entry on oaks that she'd slid under the table to prove it. "There's not enough light under here," he said. And so she finally gave in and accepted Ben, her husband, for the man he was—terribly resourceful in most situations, but under the table in a storm. "Scootch over," she said, crawling in after them as the old oak creaked but did not buckle in the buffeting.

THESE SUMMER NIGHTS IN DECEMBER

The beehive is waiting to be milked.
The cows are wondering around,
trampling the rose bushes, trying to
push their fat faces into blossoms
which fall into tatters in the process.
A small dog wanders in from the next yard,
tries to illumine its haunches
as a lightning bug lands on her forearm,
observes the glass of wine in her hand,
and barks. I light my cigar and swallow
a mouthful of chocolate pudding.
It's not the world, but how one orients
oneself towards things that's key.
I want to wash it all down
with a mouthful of pinot noir
so I lean over and kiss her perfect neck.

ME IN MY PLACE

No matter what
you're up to
the wind in the tall trees
sounds the same.

INFINITE DIVISIBILITY IS A NICE IDEA

They didn't say where they were going, they just left. Their apartment is empty except for the word "Roanoke" carved into the wall above where their bed was. Also, "That's all, folks!" written in nail polish below the door knob of their front door. They left a dictionary on the floor of the kitchen. It was the damnedest thing. In between each entry there was a tiny slit, as if made with a razor blade. As if they went looking for more words in between each word in the dictionary. As if the words there already weren't nearly enough.

ACKNOWLEDGMENTS

My thanks to the editors of the following journals and anthologies where the following poems first appeared:

Arsenic Lobster: "Emily, It's Better This Way"; "In Time To Save a Life"
Arts & Letters: "Free Verse"; "You Can Always Buy a New Dress"
B O D Y: "Apparently, I'm Not a Joiner"
Burnside Review: "Cuckold at the Zoo"
Cellpoems: "Me in My Place"
The Cincinnati Review: "In This Reality, You Exit at the Next McDonalds for Fries and a Shake"; "Infinite Divisibility Is a Nice Idea"
The Cortland Review: "Help! I'm Floating!"
Cream City Review: "Communication Problems in the Middle Ages"
Faultline: "Science Fiction Family"
Forklift, Ohio: "All Purpose, Me"; "The Wrestling Coach Taught Us Health"
Fourteen Hills: "These Summer Nights in December"
Gargoyle: "A Marriage Made on the Dining Room Floor"
Harpur Palate: "I Never Intend To, How 'Bout You?"
Inch Magazine: "Sure, You Always Land On Your Feet"
Juked: "A Look at Our Dangerous Friend"; "Being Necessary for the Maintenance of the Shimmy-Shammy"
Kill Author: "A Theme Song That Never Gets Old"
The Lumberyard: "A Little Quantum Physics Can Be Dangerous"
The Minnesota Review: "Single Male Seeks Someone Who'll Stay"; "Sword Swallowers in Transition"
NANO Fiction: "Caterpillars and Grass Snakes"; "The Exact Opposite of Exile"; "No, I Will Not Be Your Girlfriend"

Nashville Review: "If Only I'd Thought of It"

The Nervous Breakdown: "Done Playing Hard To Get"

Painted Bride Quarterly: "On Top of an Already Losing Personality"; "This Year's Will Be the Last"

Pank: "Have It Your Way"; "Lifestyle of the Non Quarterback and the Non Cheerleader"; "They Must Bake an Awful Lot of Cakes"; "Those Daring Old Men"

Paper Darts: "If You Must Know"; "Only Better (Black Moths)"

Permafrost: "She lifted her arms but she wasn't surrendering."; "The Salvation of Edna"

Poetry East: "Still Life with Plums"

Poet Lore: "Stop Doing That"

Rappahannock Review: "A Raising"

Redactions: "Typical, Really"

Scud: "New Year's Resolution TBA"

seveneightfive: "Cowboys Won't Cut It Anymore"

Spillway: "Turn Down the Thermostat, Darling"

Spout: "The Best One This Town Ever Had"

Stone Table Review: "Preparing Phoenix for Dinner"

Superstition Review: "For We, the Wide Awake"; "Homeschooling Is Really Taking Off"; "Plenty of Room Here Under the Big Top"; "A Sea Voyage and the Attendant Perspective"

Tar River Poetry: "(This Town Is) Barely Managing To Hold It To-gether"

Toad: "Ten More Minutes, Please"; "What? What Is It You're Try-ing To Tell Me?"

Zygote in My Coffee: "Love Is a Revolutionary Act"; "We Blew It and Now We Pay"

"Emily, It's Better This Way" republished in *Verse Daily*, September 4, 2009

"Happy Birthday to Me" first published as a broadside from Architrave Press and republished in the *Marie Alexander Flash Sequence Anthology*

"I Never Intend To, How 'Bout You?" republished in *Verse Daily*, November 26, 2009

"In This Reality, You Exit at the Next McDonalds for Fries and a Shake" republished in *Every River on Earth: Writing from Appalachian Ohio* edited by Neil Carpathios (Ohio University Press, Fall 2014)

"Our Apple Trees" first published as a broadside from Thrush Press

"Stop Doing That" republished as a digital broadside in *Broadsided*

Great thanks to my teachers, friends, fellow writers and family for the generosity of their support and encouragement, including Wayne Dodd, Maura Stanton, Cathy Bowman, Maurice Manning, Ross Gay, the Lawrence OPGs, J Keirn-Swanson, Dustin Nightingale, Alexander Weinstein, Joseph Citro, and Timothy Citro. Thanks also to Erika Meitner, Amy Gerstler, Marie Rosen, Tom Hunley, and the Steel Toe Books crew. Lastly, my love and thanks to Sarah Ruhlen, the Non-Cheerleader.

CHRISTOPHER CITRO holds a BA from Ohio University and an MFA from Indiana University where he received the Darrell Burton Fellowship in Creative Writing and hosted *The Poets Weave* on WFIU. His publications include poetry in *Best New Poets 2014*, *Prairie Schooner*, *Ninth Letter*, *Third Coast*, *Salt Hill*, *The Pinch* and *Verse Daily*, and creative nonfiction in *Boulevard* and *Colorado Review*. Christopher has taught creative writing at Indiana University and in the Martha's Vineyard Institute of Creative Writing, and he is the Assistant Poetry Editor for *decomP*. He lives in Syracuse, New York, with his partner, Sarah, and their black cat 92. *The Maintenance of the Shimmy-Shammy* is his first book.

www.ingramcontent.com/pod-product-compliance
Lightning Source LLC
Chambersburg PA
CBHW072044040426

42447CB00012BB/3015